Picture This

41 images to help you
solve life's problems

Nina Grunfeld

With Annie Lionnet
Illustrations by Michael Thomas

Published in 2022 by Short Books an imprint of Octopus Publishing Group Ltd
Carmelite House, 50 Victoria Embankment London, EC4Y 0DZ

www.octopusbooks.co.uk

www.shortbooks.co.uk

An Hachette UK Company

www.hachette.co.uk

Distributed in the US by Hachette Book Group, 1290 Avenue of the Americas
4th and 5th Floors New York, NY 10104

Distributed in Canada by Canadian Manda Group,
664 Annette St. Toronto, Ontario, Canada M6S 2CB

10 9 8 7 6 5 4 3 2 1

A CIP catalogue record for this book is available from the British Library.

ISBN: 978-1-78072-552-9

Illustrations copyright © Michael Thomas

Cover design by Two Associates

Printed and bound in Great Britain by Clays Ltd, Elcograf S.p.A.

This FSC® label means that materials used for the
product have been responsibly sourced

For Mike, without whom...

Welcome

We believe that, although professionals and experts can play a significant role in helping us interpret our lives, we each have a special ability to make sense of ourselves and our stories. All we need is the courage and willingness to look within ourselves and trust what we find.

The 41 images with accompanying questions will help you to explore and resolve any difficulties or challenges you might be facing, and will enable you to trust your inner wisdom so you yourself can interpret any insights you have into your thoughts and circumstances.

The key to getting the most out of *Picture This* is to be in the right frame of mind – and that's easy. Simply focus on a picture and answer the questions posed. Create an atmosphere that works for you. Some of us find it easier to concentrate if we're feeling relaxed and not under any time pressures.

We suggest using *Picture This* on your own for the first few times to familiarise yourself with the process and then sharing it with friends who may also be looking for some direction. You can work one-on-one or even in a group. It can be great fun. Be your own experiment.

How it works

1. Crystallise what you want
The first step is to think about why you are consulting the book.
Perhaps you have a specific problem with work, or relationships, or
you're in a tricky situation that needs a new perspective. Whatever
it is, try to crystallise it in your mind before you read on.

2. Get in the mood
Picture This works best when you're relaxed. Whether you're by
yourself or with others, try to get in the right zone. Maybe make a
cup of tea or put on your favourite music. Get yourself into a space
where you'll be comfortable exploring your thoughts.

3. Choose a picture
Now is the time to find the image that you are going to use to help
you. You can search for a picture you like, but we recommend the
random approach – just open the book anywhere. You never know
what you'll end up finding, so it can be more fun.

4. Read the questions
Look at the questions next to the picture. Each one has been written to
spark some connection between your situation and the image: This is
the time to open your mind and let the subconscious take over.
Why not grab a pen and paper and make some notes to help you
remember your reactions?

5. Have your 'lifebulb moment'
For some problems, *Picture This* may bring instant solutions – new
ways of thinking that crack that difficult situation open. For others, it
might take a little while – you might need to ponder for a few hours
or even a few days before the answer reveals itself.

Lifebulb moments

The seven questions that appear opposite each image in this book have been written to stimulate your imagination, to encourage or inspire you to look beyond the imagery and see how it relates to you. If you are at a turning point in your life, or have a difficult decision to make, these questions will throw a light on your situation, facilitating solutions and enabling you to clearly see your next step.

We want you to lose track of time using *Picture This*, in the same way you do when you're completely absorbed by something – deeply relaxed, totally present and in the moment. Why? Because we are often at our most creative and receptive when we are in this flow state. A 'lifebulb moment' – a sudden and spontaneous realisation about something that you haven't noticed or understood before – can often arise in these instances and have a transformational effect. They mark a turning point in our lives when we realise or decide something important.

Of course, you might not always get a life-changing result, so don't worry if it doesn't come instantly. Instead, the impact may be more subtle, and you may need to allow your intuition to cook for a while before the meaning becomes completely clear.

You can come back and look at the same image several times, asking the same question or a different one. Each time you'll gain a new perspective or insight simply by having an open mind. We recommend that you keep a record of your thoughts and responses whenever you work with an image. Write down in as much detail as possible the feelings that particular aspects of the picture evoke in you. This will enable you to keep track of both your process and your progress.

Notice coincidences

The subconscious part of the human brain is predominantly non-verbal and rich with images that elicit ideas and feelings that can trigger new trains of thought. As your mind deciphers the images in this book, associations and relationships – metaphorical or otherwise – will emerge, giving you an insight into how to view and respond to your particular situation. These spontaneous metaphors will reveal a synchronistic connection between something in your life or your inner world and the image you are looking at. Something is literally coinciding.

For example, you might look at the three jack-in-the-box (page 73) and immediately think of yourself and your two best friends or something unexpected or surprising that has happened in your life. Or you might imagine the solo flying balloon (page 21) as you escaping a difficult situation or, conversely, you feeling left out of something.

Many of the choices we make are conscious ones, but a surprising number of them remain unconscious. The pictures and questions in this book will help you connect to what is hidden from your conscious and understand the influences that shape your reality. This fresh perspective will give you much greater self-awareness, clarity and confidence.

A practice with an ancient lineage

Visual metaphors have been used throughout history in many different cultures to stimulate the imagination and change the way we think.

The ancient Chinese divination text, *I Ching* (or *Book of Changes*), for example, was written between the 10th and 4th centuries BC, and has been used for thousands of years both as a way of gaining personal insight into one's current situation and as an oracle for the future. Traditionally you 'consult' the *I Ching* by throwing yarrow sticks, or Chinese coins, which will lead you to the relevant one of 64 'hexagrams' to read and interpret.

Centuries later, ancient Greeks and Romans sought answers to questions that were bothering them by performing bibliomancy. This is a practice whereby you take a book from your collection and then, with your eyes closed, open it up at a random page, to see how your question is 'answered' by the text your finger is pointing to. Ancient scholars used to consult passages or sentences plucked at random from Homer, Virgil and other poets to gain a different perspective on a particular situation.

Tarot cards were invented in Italy in the 1430s by simply adding an extra highly illustrated suit to existing packs of playing cards. At first these cards were used to play games, but around 1780 in France they started to be used to tell fortunes. People would visit fortune tellers to have the pictures and symbols in Tarot cards interpreted for them in order to tap into their subconscious. The cards are still used like this today, not just by fortune tellers but by individuals doing the interpreting themselves.

Picture This is an exciting new concept taking the best from each of these three divination tools. We believe you will find it just as useful – if not more so.

Make this book yours

We asked two people with completely different problems to use this image (page 57) to demonstrate how *Picture This* can work.

You will see how individually they interpreted the picture and how varied their answers are. Each time you return to *Picture This* with a new question, you will find another answer to your problem, whether you use the same image or a different one.

We hope you have as many 'lifebulb moments' using *Picture This* as we have had.

Example one: partner moving abroad

1. First, decide what it is you want help with.

'I want to know whether or not I should pursue a long-distance relationship.'

2. Now look at the picture. How does it make you feel? Is there a deeper question you could be asking?

'I guess the deeper question would be whether I even have the necessary trust in me. Because of some other experiences I've had, it's often difficult for me to trust anyone. This picture makes me feel like I'm at odds with myself. It's a case of 'Am I willing to listen to my head or my heart?' To look at myself properly and decide – am I going to hold what someone did in the past against another person who's completely different?'

3. Who or what are you in the picture?

'The top magnet is my head and the bottom one is my heart, and I need to take that final step to put the two magnets together.'

4. Who or what else from your life is in the picture?

'The white space around is my partner. He's surrounding both my head and my heart, and he is also what is keeping the space between everything.'

5. How can this picture help?

'It has made me realise that this is just me fighting myself, rather than there being something external stopping me. I think the long-distance problem is just me making excuses.'

6. What would you like to add or take away from the picture?

'I want to get rid of the head magnet and just follow my heart. But that's very difficult for me to do.'

7. What's next?

'I've realised that I need to do some work on myself first as I don't have the trust to commit to a relationship. I think it would be unfair to him to keep doing what I'm doing, so it's maybe about getting that space from him and focusing on my own wellbeing right now.'

Example two: having a difficult time

1. First, decide what it is you want help with.
'I want to understand why these last few years have been so bad for me.'

2. Now look at the picture. How does it make you feel? Is there a deeper question you could be asking?
'When I look at the picture, I immediately think of horseshoes – how horseshoes can be lucky or unlucky depending on how you place them. It makes me think of my best friend, who's had such good luck these past few years, and maybe that I'm a bit jealous of that. I want to know how I can be more positive in my outlook on life.'

3. Who or what are you in the picture?
'I feel like I'm the top horseshoe and all my luck has fallen into the bottom horseshoe.'

4. Who or what else from your life is in the picture?
'The bottom horseshoe would be my friend, who has everything going right for them. They're the lucky horseshoe, collecting all the luck.'

5. How can this picture help?
'I can see that if I turn the book sideways, the horseshoes aren't on top of each other – they are both lying sideways, one next to the other. That would mean we'd both have the same amount of luck, good and bad.'

6. What would you like to add or take away from the picture?
'I don't think it's a case of adding or taking away anything, it's just turning the page on its side. Then I can look at the problem with a different perspective and try and work from there.'

7. What's next?
'I think I need to speak to my friend and focus on not being bitter or holding anything against them. Their good luck isn't because of my bad luck, it's just how the world works. Luck will swing my way eventually.'

Over to you

Remember, whatever method you choose to use in your search for insight, the secret is to be intuitive and receptive and allow the words or images to help you find the answers you are looking for. When using *Picture This*, trust your feelings.

We very much hope you enjoy using this book and will do so for years.

The questions below will guide your thinking. If it helps, get a pad of paper and write down your answers – remember to date them.

1. First, decide on what it is you want help with.
Is there a tricky situation you'd like resolving? Or are you looking for a moment of clarity?

2. Now look at the picture. How does it make you feel?
Does it reflect your situation? Or does it make you think there's a deeper question you could be asking?

3. Who or what are you in the picture?
You choose. You can be anything from the man to the hands shaking. You can even be on the ceiling looking down.

4. Who or what else from your life is in the picture?
Find each of the elements of your situation in the picture. Trust your intuition. Don't judge your decisions.

5. How can this picture help?
Now you've decided what everything is in the picture, think about how it might help you see the situation differently. Think laterally.

6. What would you like to add or take away from the picture?
For example, you could add a door, change the size of the man or remove him entirely.

7. What's next?
Decide on one simple thing you can do in the next seven days that will inspire you to move forward. Write this goal somewhere you'll remember.

The questions below will guide your thinking. If it helps, get a pad of paper and write down your answers – remember to date them.

1. First, decide on what it is you want help with.
Is there a tricky situation you'd like resolving? Or are you looking for a moment of clarity?

2. Now look at the picture. How does it make you feel?
Does it reflect your situation? Or does it make you think there's a deeper question you could be asking?

3. Who or what are you in the picture?
You choose. You can be anything, from the alarm bell to one of the dropped hands. You can even be looking at the clock from outside the picture.

4. Who or what else from your life is in the picture?
Find each of the elements of your situation in the picture. Trust your intuition. Don't judge your decisions.

5. How can this picture help?
Now you've decided what everything is in the picture, think about how it might help you see the situation differently. Think laterally.

6. What would you like to add or take away from the picture?
For example, you could put a smiley face on the clock, paint clouds on the wall behind or replace the clock with a cockerel.

7. What's next?
Decide on one simple thing you can do in the next seven days that will inspire you to move forward. Write this goal somewhere you'll remember.

The questions below will guide your thinking. If it helps, get a pad of paper and write down your answers – remember to date them.

1. First, decide on what it is you want help with.
Is there a tricky situation you'd like resolving? Or are you looking for a moment of clarity?

2. Now look at the picture. How does it make you feel?
Does it reflect your situation? Or does it make you think there's a deeper question you could be asking?

3. Who or what are you in the picture?
You choose. You can be anything from the person inside the wrapping to the string or you could be outside the picture looking in.

4. Who or what else from your life is in the picture?
Find each of the elements of your situation in the picture. Trust your intuition. Don't judge your decisions.

5. How can this picture help?
Now you've decided what everything is in the picture, think about how it might help you see the situation differently. Think laterally.

6. What would you like to add or take away from the picture?
For example, you could add a pair of scissors, change the paper to gift wrap or just turn the person around. Maybe the back isn't wrapped up.

7. What's next?
Decide on one simple thing you can do in the next seven days that will inspire you to move forward. Write this goal somewhere you'll remember.

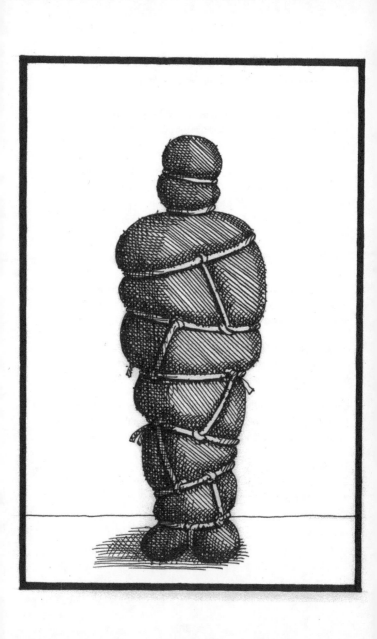

The questions below will guide your thinking. If it helps, get a pad of paper and write down your answers – remember to date them.

1. First, decide on what it is you want help with.
Is there a tricky situation you'd like resolving? Or are you looking for a moment of clarity?

2. Now look at the picture. How does it make you feel?
Does it reflect your situation? Or does it make you think there's a deeper question you could be asking?

3. Who or what are you in the picture?
You choose. You can be anything, from the hand holding the balloons or the balloon floating free. You can even be the sky.

4. Who or what else from your life is in the picture?
Find each of the elements of your situation in the picture. Trust your intuition. Don't judge your decisions.

5. How can this picture help?
Now you've decided what everything is in the picture, think about how it might help you see the situation differently. Think laterally.

6. What would you like to add or take away from the picture?
For example, you could burst all the balloons, let them all fly away, or add a bench you could tie them to so you could walk away.

7. What's next?
Decide on one simple thing you can do in the next seven days that will inspire you to move forward. Write this goal somewhere you'll remember.

The questions below will guide your thinking. If it helps, get a pad of paper and write down your answers – remember to date them.

1. First, decide on what it is you want help with.
Is there a tricky situation you'd like resolving? Or are you looking for a moment of clarity?

2. Now look at the picture. How does it make you feel?
Does it reflect your situation? Or does it make you think there's a deeper question you could be asking?

3. Who or what are you in the picture?
You choose. You can be anything from the shaft of light to the knob on the door. You could even be outside the room looking in.

4. Who or what else from your life is in the picture?
Find each of the elements of your situation in the picture. Trust your intuition. Don't judge your decisions.

5. How can this picture help?
Now you've decided what everything is in the picture, think about how it might help you see the situation differently. Think laterally.

6. What would you like to add or take away from the picture?
For example, you could open the door fully or even remove the walls, add a window or have someone walk into the room.

7. What's next?
Decide on one simple thing you can do in the next seven days that will inspire you to move forward. Write this goal somewhere you'll remember.

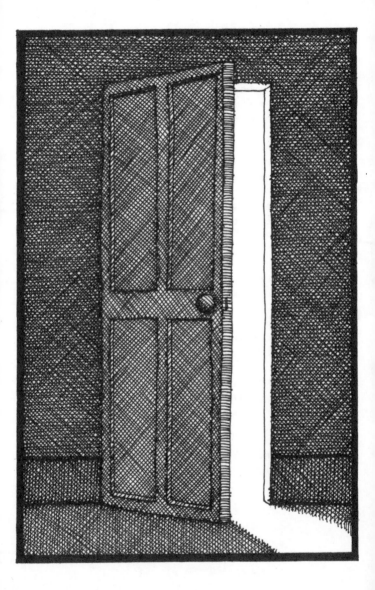

The questions below will guide your thinking. If it helps, get a pad of paper and write down your answers – remember to date them.

1. First, decide on what it is you want help with.
Is there a tricky situation you'd like resolving? Or are you looking for a moment of clarity?

2. Now look at the picture. How does it make you feel?
Does it reflect your situation? Or does it make you think there's a deeper question you could be asking?

3. Who or what are you in the picture?
You choose. You can be anything from the woman to the target to the arrow. You can even be firing the arrow.

4. Who or what else from your life is in the picture?
Find each of the elements of your situation in the picture. Trust your intuition. Don't judge your decisions.

5. How can this picture help?
Now you've decided what everything is in the picture, think about how it might help you see the situation differently. Think laterally.

6. What would you like to add or take away from the picture?
For example, you could change the direction of the arrow, put the arrow in the bullseye or remove the woman entirely.

7. What's next?
Decide on one simple thing you can do in the next seven days that will inspire you to move forward. Write this goal somewhere you'll remember.

The questions below will guide your thinking. If it helps, get a pad of paper and write down your answers – remember to date them.

1. First, decide on what it is you want help with.
Is there a tricky situation you'd like resolving? Or are you looking for a moment of clarity?

2. Now look at the picture. How does it make you feel?
Does it reflect your situation? Or does it make you think there's a deeper question you could be asking?

3. Who or what are you in the picture?
You choose. You can be anything from the wild sea to the girls. You can even be the space between the cliffs.

4. Who or what else from your life is in the picture?
Find each of the elements of your situation in the picture. Trust your intuition. Don't judge your decisions.

5. How can this picture help?
Now you've decided what everything is in the picture, think about how it might help you see the situation differently. Think laterally.

6. What would you like to add or take away from the picture?
For example, you could add a bridge, make the sea calm, join the cliffs together or bring in a helicopter.

7. What's next?
Decide on one simple thing you can do in the next seven days that will inspire you to move forward. Write this goal somewhere you'll remember.

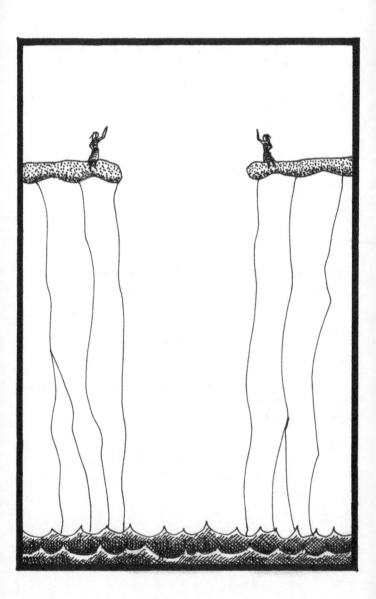

The questions below will guide your thinking. If it helps, get a pad of paper and write down your answers – remember to date them.

1. First, decide on what it is you want help with.
Is there a tricky situation you'd like resolving? Or are you looking for a moment of clarity?

2. Now look at the picture. How does it make you feel?
Does it reflect your situation? Or does it make you think there's a deeper question you could be asking?

3. Who or what are you in the picture?
You choose. You can be anything from the door to the stairs or even the brick wall.

4. Who or what else from your life is in the picture?
Find each of the elements of your situation in the picture. Trust your intuition. Don't judge your decisions.

5. How can this picture help?
Now you've decided what everything is in the picture, think about how it might help you see the situation differently. Think laterally.

6. What would you like to add or take away from the picture?
For example, you could move the door or the stairs, turn the bricks into glass and add a few people coming out of the door.

7. What's next?
Decide on one simple thing you can do in the next seven days that will inspire you to move forward. Write this goal somewhere you'll remember.

The questions below will guide your thinking. If it helps, get a pad of paper and write down your answers – remember to date them.

1. First, decide on what it is you want help with.
Is there a tricky situation you'd like resolving? Or are you looking for a moment of clarity?

2. Now look at the picture. How does it make you feel?
Does it reflect your situation? Or does it make you think there's a deeper question you could be asking?

3. Who or what are you in the picture?
You choose. You can be anything from the handle to a hole in the umbrella. You can even be outside the picture looking in.

4. Who or what else from your life is in the picture?
Find each of the elements of your situation in the picture. Trust your intuition. Don't judge your decisions.

5. How can this picture help?
Now you've decided what everything is in the picture, think about how it might help you see the situation differently. Think laterally.

6. What would you like to add or take away from the picture?
For example, you could sew up the holes, make it a sunny day or add some raindrops.

7. What's next?
Decide on one simple thing you can do in the next seven days that will inspire you to move forward. Write this goal somewhere you'll remember.

The questions below will guide your thinking. If it helps, get a pad of paper and write down your answers – remember to date them.

1. First, decide on what it is you want help with.
Is there a tricky situation you'd like resolving? Or are you looking for a moment of clarity?

2. Now look at the picture. How does it make you feel?
Does it reflect your situation? Or does it make you think there's a deeper question you could be asking?

3. Who or what are you in the picture?
You choose. You can be anything from the biggest fish to the worm. You can even be the sea.

4. Who or what else from your life is in the picture?
Find each of the elements of your situation in the picture. Trust your intuition. Don't judge your decisions.

5. How can this picture help?
Now you've decided what everything is in the picture, think about how it might help you see the situation differently. Think laterally.

6. What would you like to add or take away from the picture?
For example, you could remove the hook and line entirely, add a net to catch one or more of the fish or remove the largest two fish.

7. What's next?
Decide on one simple thing you can do in the next seven days that will inspire you to move forward. Write this goal somewhere you'll remember.

The questions below will guide your thinking. If it helps, get a pad of paper and write down your answers – remember to date them.

1. First, decide on what it is you want help with.
Is there a tricky situation you'd like resolving? Or are you looking for a moment of clarity?

2. Now look at the picture. How does it make you feel?
Does it reflect your situation? Or does it make you think there's a deeper question you could be asking?

3. Who or what are you in the picture?
You choose. You can be anything from either of the women to the ceiling or the white space.

4. Who or what else from your life is in the picture?
Find each of the elements of your situation in the picture. Trust your intuition. Don't judge your decisions.

5. How can this picture help?
Now you've decided what everything is in the picture, think about how it might help you see the situation differently. Think laterally.

6. What would you like to add or take away from the picture?
For example, you could bring the woman on the ceiling down, add a few more people or a chair.

7. What's next?
Decide on one simple thing you can do in the next seven days that will inspire you to move forward. Write this goal somewhere you'll remember.

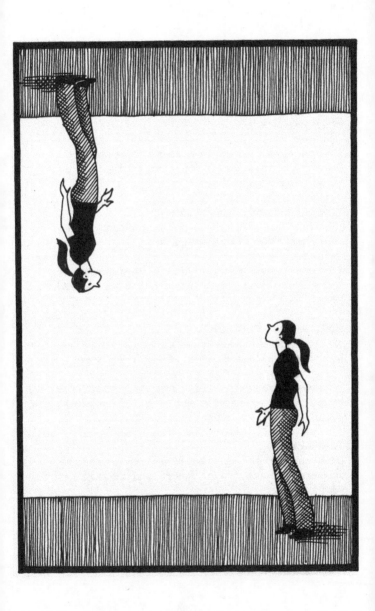

*The questions below will guide your thinking. If it helps, get a pad
of paper and write down your answers – remember to date them.*

1. First, decide on what it is you want help with.

Is there a tricky situation you'd like resolving? Or are you looking
for a moment of clarity?

2. Now look at the picture. How does it make you feel?

Does it reflect your situation? Or does it make you think there's a
deeper question you could be asking?

3. Who or what are you in the picture?

You choose. You can be anything from the empty space in the
brain to one of the pieces of jigsaw puzzle.

4. Who or what else from your life is in the picture?

Find each of the elements of your situation in the picture. Trust your
intuition. Don't judge your decisions.

5. How can this picture help?

Now you've decided what everything is in the picture, think about
how it might help you see the situation differently. Think laterally.

6. What would you like to add or take away from the picture?

For example, you could paint the entire head black, remove the jigsaw
puzzle pieces or turn the person's head around.

7. What's next?

Decide on one simple thing you can do in the next seven days that
will inspire you to move forward. Write this goal somewhere
you'll remember.

The questions below will guide your thinking. If it helps, get a pad of paper and write down your answers – remember to date them.

1. First, decide on what it is you want help with.
Is there a tricky situation you'd like resolving? Or are you looking for a moment of clarity?

2. Now look at the picture. How does it make you feel?
Does it reflect your situation? Or does it make you think there's a deeper question you could be asking?

3. Who or what are you in the picture?
You choose. You can be anything from the scissors to one of the blades or a link in the chain.

4. Who or what else from your life is in the picture?
Find each of the elements of your situation in the picture. Trust your intuition. Don't judge your decisions.

5. How can this picture help?
Now you've decided what everything is in the picture, think about how it might help you see the situation differently. Think laterally.

6. What would you like to add or take away from the picture?
For example, you could change what the chain is made of or add a person holding the scissors.

7. What's next?
Decide on one simple thing you can do in the next seven days that will inspire you to move forward. Write this goal somewhere you'll remember.

The questions below will guide your thinking. If it helps, get a pad of paper and write down your answers – remember to date them.

1. First, decide on what it is you want help with.
Is there a tricky situation you'd like resolving? Or are you looking for a moment of clarity?

2. Now look at the picture. How does it make you feel?
Does it reflect your situation? Or does it make you think there's a deeper question you could be asking?

3. Who or what are you in the picture?
You choose. You can be anything from the woman to the reflection, or both of them. You can even be the mirror itself.

4. Who or what else from your life is in the picture?
Find each of the elements of your situation in the picture. Trust your intuition. Don't judge your decisions.

5. How can this picture help?
Now you've decided what everything is in the picture, think about how it might help you see the situation differently. Think laterally.

6. What would you like to add or take away from the picture?
For example, you could take the mirror away, turn the reflection around or remove the woman.

7. What's next?
Decide on one simple thing you can do in the next seven days that will inspire you to move forward. Write this goal somewhere you'll remember.

The questions below will guide your thinking. If it helps, get a pad of paper and write down your answers – remember to date them.

1. First, decide on what it is you want help with.
Is there a tricky situation you'd like resolving? Or are you looking for a moment of clarity?

2. Now look at the picture. How does it make you feel?
Does it reflect your situation? Or does it make you think there's a deeper question you could be asking?

3. Who or what are you in the picture?
You choose. You can be one of the four lines of rope or the knot. You can even be on the ceiling looking down.

4. Who or what else from your life is in the picture?
Find each of the elements of your situation in the picture. Trust your intuition. Don't judge your decisions.

5. How can this picture help?
Now you've decided what everything is in the picture, think about how it might help you see the situation differently. Think laterally.

6. What would you like to add or take away from the picture?
For example, you could zoom out of the picture to see how small the knot is, or you could change its texture or pull the four strands to see if it unravels.

7. What's next?
Decide on one simple thing you can do in the next seven days that will inspire you to move forward. Write this goal somewhere you'll remember.

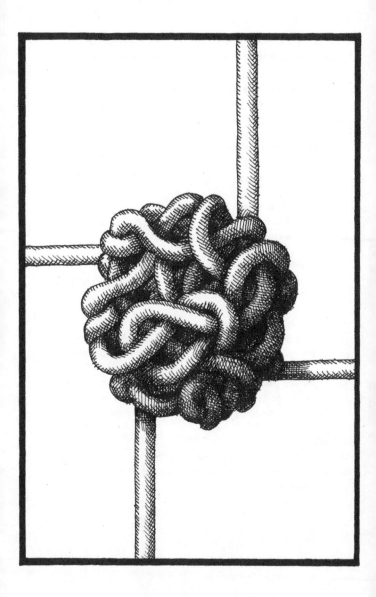

The questions below will guide your thinking. If it helps, get a pad of paper and write down your answers – remember to date them.

1. First, decide on what it is you want help with.
Is there a tricky situation you'd like resolving? Or are you looking for a moment of clarity?

2. Now look at the picture. How does it make you feel?
Does it reflect your situation? Or does it make you think there's a deeper question you could be asking?

3. Who or what are you in the picture?
You choose. You can be anything from the five-fingered glove to a thumb on one of the gloves or even the stitching around the cuff.

4. Who or what else from your life is in the picture?
Find each of the elements of your situation in the picture. Trust your intuition. Don't judge your decisions.

5. How can this picture help?
Now you've decided what everything is in the picture, think about how it might help you see the situation differently. Think laterally.

6. What would you like to add or take away from the picture?
For example, you could add hands that fit the gloves, or draw in or remove fingers from the gloves to make them the same.

7. What's next?
Decide on one simple thing you can do in the next seven days that will inspire you to move forward. Write this goal somewhere you'll remember.

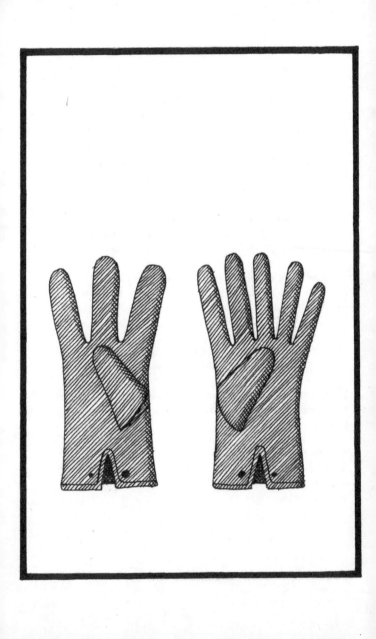

The questions below will guide your thinking. If it helps, get a pad of paper and write down your answers – remember to date them.

1. First, decide on what it is you want help with.
Is there a tricky situation you'd like resolving? Or are you looking for a moment of clarity?

2. Now look at the picture. How does it make you feel?
Does it reflect your situation? Or does it make you think there's a deeper question you could be asking?

3. Who or what are you in the picture?
You choose. You can be anything from the woman to the square wheel or the juggling balls. You can even be on a bike next to her.

4. Who or what else from your life is in the picture?
Find each of the elements of your situation in the picture. Trust your intuition. Don't judge your decisions.

5. How can this picture help?
Now you've decided what everything is in the picture, think about how it might help you see the situation differently. Think laterally.

6. What would you like to add or take away from the picture?
For example, you could make the wheel round, or remove the balls or the bicycle.

7. What's next?
Decide on one simple thing you can do in the next seven days that will inspire you to move forward. Write this goal somewhere you'll remember.

The questions below will guide your thinking. If it helps, get a pad of paper and write down your answers – remember to date them.

1. First, decide on what it is you want help with.
Is there a tricky situation you'd like resolving? Or are you looking for a moment of clarity?

2. Now look at the picture. How does it make you feel?
Does it reflect your situation? Or does it make you think there's a deeper question you could be asking?

3. Who or what are you in the picture?
You choose. You can be anything from the man rubbing the lamp to the lamp itself or even the smoke.

4. Who or what else from your life is in the picture?
Find each of the elements of your situation in the picture. Trust your intuition. Don't judge your decisions.

5. How can this picture help?
Now you've decided what everything is in the picture, think about how it might help you see the situation differently. Think laterally.

6. What would you like to add or take away from the picture?
For example, someone you know might be coming out of the lamp or the man might be in a different landscape.

7. What's next?
Decide on one simple thing you can do in the next seven days that will inspire you to move forward. Write this goal somewhere you'll remember.

The questions below will guide your thinking. If it helps, get a pad of paper and write down your answers – remember to date them.

1. First, decide on what it is you want help with.
Is there a tricky situation you'd like resolving? Or are you looking for a moment of clarity?

2. Now look at the picture. How does it make you feel?
Does it reflect your situation? Or does it make you think there's a deeper question you could be asking?

3. Who or what are you in the picture?
You choose. You can be anything from the woman to the dove to the worm. You can be opposite the woman watching the scene.

4. Who or what else from your life is in the picture?
Find each of the elements of your situation in the picture. Trust your intuition. Don't judge your decisions.

5. How can this picture help?
Now you've decided what everything is in the picture, think about how it might help you see the situation differently. Think laterally.

6. What would you like to add or take away from the picture?
For example, you could remove the nest from the woman's head, have the chicks fly the nest or open the woman's eyes.

7. What's next?
Decide on one simple thing you can do in the next seven days that will inspire you to move forward. Write this goal somewhere you'll remember.

The questions below will guide your thinking. If it helps, get a pad of paper and write down your answers – remember to date them.

1. First, decide on what it is you want help with.
Is there a tricky situation you'd like resolving? Or are you looking for a moment of clarity?

2. Now look at the picture. How does it make you feel?
Does it reflect your situation? Or does it make you think there's a deeper question you could be asking?

3. Who or what are you in the picture?
You choose. You can be anything from the bowl to the water or even one of the fish.

4. Who or what else from your life is in the picture?
Find each of the elements of your situation in the picture. Trust your intuition. Don't judge your decisions.

5. How can this picture help?
Now you've decided what everything is in the picture, think about how it might help you see the situation differently. Think laterally.

6. What would you like to add or take away from the picture?
For example, you could use a net to put the second fish in the bowl or add more fish or you could replace the bowl with an aquarium.

7. What's next?
Decide on one simple thing you can do in the next seven days that will inspire you to move forward. Write this goal somewhere you'll remember.

The questions below will guide your thinking. If it helps, get a pad of paper and write down your answers – remember to date them.

1. First, decide on what it is you want help with.
Is there a tricky situation you'd like resolving? Or are you looking for a moment of clarity?

2. Now look at the picture. How does it make you feel?
Does it reflect your situation? Or does it make you think there's a deeper question you could be asking?

3. Who or what are you in the picture?
You choose. You can be anything from the woman to the crack in the floor to the pearl necklace. You can even be standing on the wider part of the crack.

4. Who or what else from your life is in the picture?
Find each of the elements of your situation in the picture. Trust your intuition. Don't judge your decisions.

5. How can this picture help?
Now you've decided what everything is in the picture, think about how it might help you see the situation differently. Think laterally.

6. What would you like to add or take away from the picture?
For example, you could close the crack, make the woman jump away from it or remove her entirely.

7. What's next?
Decide on one simple thing you can do in the next seven days that will inspire you to move forward. Write this goal somewhere you'll remember.

The questions below will guide your thinking. If it helps, get a pad of paper and write down your answers – remember to date them.

1. First, decide on what it is you want help with.
Is there a tricky situation you'd like resolving? Or are you looking for a moment of clarity?

2. Now look at the picture. How does it make you feel?
Does it reflect your situation? Or does it make you think there's a deeper question you could be asking?

3. Who or what are you in the picture?
You choose. You can be one of the magnets, or the surface they're lying on or the force between them.

4. Who or what else from your life is in the picture?
Find each of the elements of your situation in the picture. Trust your intuition. Don't judge your decisions.

5. How can this picture help?
Now you've decided what everything is in the picture, think about how it might help you see the situation differently. Think laterally.

6. What would you like to add or take away from the picture?
For example, you could turn one of the magnets around, hide one of them or bring in some iron filings.

7. What's next?
Decide on one simple thing you can do in the next seven days that will inspire you to move forward. Write this goal somewhere you'll remember.

The questions below will guide your thinking. If it helps, get a pad of paper and write down your answers – remember to date them.

1. First, decide on what it is you want help with.
Is there a tricky situation you'd like resolving? Or are you looking for a moment of clarity?

2. Now look at the picture. How does it make you feel?
Does it reflect your situation? Or does it make you think there's a deeper question you could be asking?

3. Who or what are you in the picture?
You choose. You can be anything from the saucer to the man to the teapot.

4. Who or what else from your life is in the picture?
Find each of the elements of your situation in the picture. Trust your intuition. Don't judge your decisions.

5. How can this picture help?
Now you've decided what everything is in the picture, think about how it might help you see the situation differently. Think laterally.

6. What would you like to add or take away from the picture?
For example, you could have the teapot pouring tea into the cup, remove both the people or replace the teapot and cup with faces.

7. What's next?
Decide on one simple thing you can do in the next seven days that will inspire you to move forward. Write this goal somewhere you'll remember.

The questions below will guide your thinking. If it helps, get a pad of paper and write down your answers – remember to date them.

1. First, decide on what it is you want help with.
Is there a tricky situation you'd like resolving? Or are you looking for a moment of clarity?

2. Now look at the picture. How does it make you feel?
Does it reflect your situation? Or does it make you think there's a deeper question you could be asking?

3. Who or what are you in the picture?
You choose. You can be anything from the woman to the white wall or the shadow.

4. Who or what else from your life is in the picture?
Find each of the elements of your situation in the picture. Trust your intuition. Don't judge your decisions.

5. How can this picture help?
Now you've decided what everything is in the picture, think about how it might help you see the situation differently. Think laterally.

6. What would you like to add or take away from the picture?
For example, you could turn the woman around, move the light source so there's no longer a shadow or bring another person in to walk with her.

7. What's next?
Decide on one simple thing you can do in the next seven days that will inspire you to move forward. Write this goal somewhere you'll remember.

The questions below will guide your thinking. If it helps, get a pad of paper and write down your answers – remember to date them.

1. First, decide on what it is you want help with.
Is there a tricky situation you'd like resolving? Or are you looking for a moment of clarity?

2. Now look at the picture. How does it make you feel?
Does it reflect your situation? Or does it make you think there's a deeper question you could be asking?

3. Who or what are you in the picture?
You choose. You can be anything from the little bird to the cage within the cage or the ring at the top of the bigger cage.

4. Who or what else from your life is in the picture?
Find each of the elements of your situation in the picture. Trust your intuition. Don't judge your decisions.

5. How can this picture help?
Now you've decided what everything is in the picture, think about how it might help you see the situation differently. Think laterally.

6. What would you like to add or take away from the picture?
For example, you could make the little bird fly away, make its cage much bigger or remove both cages.

7. What's next?
Decide on one simple thing you can do in the next seven days that will inspire you to move forward. Write this goal somewhere you'll remember.

The questions below will guide your thinking. If it helps, get a pad of paper and write down your answers – remember to date them.

1. First, decide on what it is you want help with.
Is there a tricky situation you'd like resolving? Or are you looking for a moment of clarity?

2. Now look at the picture. How does it make you feel?
Does it reflect your situation? Or does it make you think there's a deeper question you could be asking?

3. Who or what are you in the picture?
You choose. You can be anything from the diver to the bowl of water or the floor.

4. Who or what else from your life is in the picture?
Find each of the elements of your situation in the picture. Trust your intuition. Don't judge your decisions.

5. How can this picture help?
Now you've decided what everything is in the picture, think about how it might help you see the situation differently. Think laterally.

6. What would you like to add or take away from the picture?
For example, you could add a swimming pool, give the diver a jet pack so she could fly upwards or give her a deckchair to sit on.

7. What's next?
Decide on one simple thing you can do in the next seven days that will inspire you to move forward. Write this goal somewhere you'll remember.

The questions below will guide your thinking. If it helps, get a pad of paper and write down your answers – remember to date them.

1. First, decide on what it is you want help with.

Is there a tricky situation you'd like resolving? Or are you looking for a moment of clarity?

2. Now look at the picture. How does it make you feel?

Does it reflect your situation? Or does it make you think there's a deeper question you could be asking?

3. Who or what are you in the picture?

You choose. You can be anything from the open chrysalis to the butterfly to one of the twigs.

4. Who or what else from your life is in the picture?

Find each of the elements of your situation in the picture. Trust your intuition. Don't judge your decisions.

5. How can this picture help?

Now you've decided what everything is in the picture, think about how it might help you see the situation differently. Think laterally.

6. What would you like to add or take away from the picture?

For example, you might want to make the butterfly fly away or go back in its chrysalis, or make the woman walk.

7. What's next?

Decide on one simple thing you can do in the next seven days that will inspire you to move forward. Write this goal somewhere you'll remember.

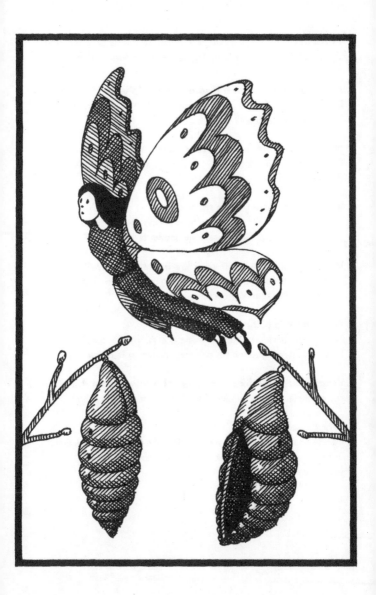

The questions below will guide your thinking. If it helps, get a pad of paper and write down your answers – remember to date them.

1. First, decide on what it is you want help with.
Is there a tricky situation you'd like resolving? Or are you looking for a moment of clarity?

2. Now look at the picture. How does it make you feel?
Does it reflect your situation? Or does it make you think there's a deeper question you could be asking?

3. Who or what are you in the picture?
You choose. You can be anything from the man or the woman or you could be one of the arches or the ladder or in a plane flying over.

4. Who or what else from your life is in the picture?
Find each of the elements of your situation in the picture. Trust your intuition. Don't judge your decisions.

5. How can this picture help?
Now you've decided what everything is in the picture, think about how it might help you see the situation differently. Think laterally.

6. What would you like to add or take away from the picture?
For example, you could remove the ladders or the wall entirely.

7. What's next?
Decide on one simple thing you can do in the next seven days that will inspire you to move forward. Write this goal somewhere you'll remember.

The questions below will guide your thinking. If it helps, get a pad of paper and write down your answers – remember to date them.

1. First, decide on what it is you want help with.
Is there a tricky situation you'd like resolving? Or are you looking for a moment of clarity?

2. Now look at the picture. How does it make you feel?
Does it reflect your situation? Or does it make you think there's a deeper question you could be asking?

3. Who or what are you in the picture?
You choose. You can be anything from the woman to the cloud. You can even be the view from above the cloud looking down.

4. Who or what else from your life is in the picture?
Find each of the elements of your situation in the picture. Trust your intuition. Don't judge your decisions.

5. How can this picture help?
Now you've decided what everything is in the picture, think about how it might help you see the situation differently. Think laterally.

6. What would you like to add or take away from the picture?
For example, you could make the cloud rain, bring in some wind to blow it away or move the woman from under it.

7. What's next?
Decide on one simple thing you can do in the next seven days that will inspire you to move forward. Write this goal somewhere you'll remember.

The questions below will guide your thinking. If it helps, get a pad of paper and write down your answers – remember to date them.

1. First, decide on what it is you want help with.
Is there a tricky situation you'd like resolving? Or are you looking for a moment of clarity?

2. Now look at the picture. How does it make you feel?
Does it reflect your situation? Or does it make you think there's a deeper question you could be asking?

3. Who or what are you in the picture?
You choose. You can be the closed box or the smiling head of the second jack-in-the-box or the invisible hand operating them.

4. Who or what else from your life is in the picture?
Find each of the elements of your situation in the picture. Trust your intuition. Don't judge your decisions.

5. How can this picture help?
Now you've decided what everything is in the picture, think about how it might help you see the situation differently. Think laterally.

6. What would you like to add or take away from the picture?
For example, you could open the third box, or put the head back on the middle jack-in-the-box or close the first box.

7. What's next?
Decide on one simple thing you can do in the next seven days that will inspire you to move forward. Write this goal somewhere you'll remember.

The questions below will guide your thinking. If it helps, get a pad of paper and write down your answers – remember to date them.

1. First, decide on what it is you want help with.
Is there a tricky situation you'd like resolving? Or are you looking for a moment of clarity?

2. Now look at the picture. How does it make you feel?
Does it reflect your situation? Or does it make you think there's a deeper question you could be asking?

3. Who or what are you in the picture?
You choose. You can be anything from the man to the net to the star.

4. Who or what else from your life is in the picture?
Find each of the elements of your situation in the picture. Trust your intuition. Don't judge your decisions.

5. How can this picture help?
Now you've decided what everything is in the picture, think about how it might help you see the situation differently. Think laterally.

6. What would you like to add or take away from the picture?
For example, you could make the net bigger, bring the star in closer or add more people with nets.

7. What's next?
Decide on one simple thing you can do in the next seven days that will inspire you to move forward. Write this goal somewhere you'll remember.

The questions below will guide your thinking. If it helps, get a pad of paper and write down your answers – remember to date them.

1. First, decide on what it is you want help with.
Is there a tricky situation you'd like resolving? Or are you looking for a moment of clarity?

2. Now look at the picture. How does it make you feel?
Does it reflect your situation? Or does it make you think there's a deeper question you could be asking?

3. Who or what are you in the picture?
You choose. You can be anything from the choppy sea to the bright light of the lighthouse or one of the boats.

4. Who or what else from your life is in the picture?
Find each of the elements of your situation in the picture. Trust your intuition. Don't judge your decisions.

5. How can this picture help?
Now you've decided what everything is in the picture, think about how it might help you see the situation differently. Think laterally.

6. What would you like to add or take away from the picture?
For example, you could remove the storm clouds so the sun can shine or right all the boats in the sea.

7. What's next?
Decide on one simple thing you can do in the next seven days that will inspire you to move forward. Write this goal somewhere you'll remember.

The questions below will guide your thinking. If it helps, get a pad of paper and write down your answers – remember to date them.

1. First, decide on what it is you want help with.
Is there a tricky situation you'd like resolving? Or are you looking for a moment of clarity?

2. Now look at the picture. How does it make you feel?
Does it reflect your situation? Or does it make you think there's a deeper question you could be asking?

3. Who or what are you in the picture?
You choose. You can be anything from the woman to the apple or the timebomb. You can even be watching the woman from across the room.

4. Who or what else from your life is in the picture?
Find each of the elements of your situation in the picture. Trust your intuition. Don't judge your decisions.

5. How can this picture help?
Now you've decided what everything is in the picture, think about how it might help you see the situation differently. Think laterally.

6. What would you like to add or take away from the picture?
For example, you could throw the timebomb, or remove it entirely or you could open the woman's eyes.

7. What's next?
Decide on one simple thing you can do in the next seven days that will inspire you to move forward. Write this goal somewhere you'll remember.

The questions below will guide your thinking. If it helps, get a pad of paper and write down your answers — remember to date them.

1. First, decide on what it is you want help with.
Is there a tricky situation you'd like resolving? Or are you looking for a moment of clarity?

2. Now look at the picture. How does it make you feel?
Does it reflect your situation? Or does it make you think there's a deeper question you could be asking?

3. Who or what are you in the picture?
You choose. You can be anything from the stork to the sling or one of the children or even a cloud.

4. Who or what else from your life is in the picture?
Find each of the elements of your situation in the picture. Trust your intuition. Don't judge your decisions.

5. How can this picture help?
Now you've decided what everything is in the picture, think about how it might help you see the situation differently. Think laterally.

6. What would you like to add or take away from the picture?
For example, you could add another person to the sling or have the stork landing on the ground or the clouds blown away.

7. What's next?
Decide on one simple thing you can do in the next seven days that will inspire you to move forward. Write this goal somewhere you'll remember.

The questions below will guide your thinking. If it helps, get a pad of paper and write down your answers – remember to date them.

1. First, decide on what it is you want help with.
Is there a tricky situation you'd like resolving? Or are you looking for a moment of clarity?

2. Now look at the picture. How does it make you feel?
Does it reflect your situation? Or does it make you think there's a deeper question you could be asking?

3. Who or what are you in the picture?
You choose. You can be either or both of the two people, or the shadows. You can even be outside the room looking in.

4. Who or what else from your life is in the picture?
Find each of the elements of your situation in the picture. Trust your intuition. Don't judge your decisions.

5. How can this picture help?
Now you've decided what everything is in the picture, think about how it might help you see the situation differently. Think laterally.

6. What would you like to add or take away from the picture?
For example, you could stop the person on the left leaving, you could remove the walls or have both people outdoors.

7. What's next?
Decide on one simple thing you can do in the next seven days that will inspire you to move forward. Write this goal somewhere you'll remember.

The questions below will guide your thinking. If it helps, get a pad of paper and write down your answers – remember to date them.

1. First, decide on what it is you want help with.
Is there a tricky situation you'd like resolving? Or are you looking for a moment of clarity?

2. Now look at the picture. How does it make you feel?
Does it reflect your situation? Or does it make you think there's a deeper question you could be asking?

3. Who or what are you in the picture?
You choose. You can be anything from the woman holding the book to the floating pages. You can even be standing opposite her watching it all.

4. Who or what else from your life is in the picture?
Find each of the elements of your situation in the picture. Trust your intuition. Don't judge your decisions.

5. How can this picture help?
Now you've decided what everything is in the picture, think about how it might help you see the situation differently. Think laterally.

6. What would you like to add or take away from the picture?
For example, you could put the pages back in the book, remove the woman's spectacles or give her a new book.

7. What's next?
Decide on one simple thing you can do in the next seven days that will inspire you to move forward. Write this goal somewhere you'll remember.

The questions below will guide your thinking. If it helps, get a pad of paper and write down your answers – remember to date them.

1. First, decide on what it is you want help with.
Is there a tricky situation you'd like resolving? Or are you looking for a moment of clarity?

2. Now look at the picture. How does it make you feel?
Does it reflect your situation? Or does it make you think there's a deeper question you could be asking?

3. Who or what are you in the picture?
You choose. You can be the scarecrow, or one of the crows, or the top hat or even the trees watching the scene from afar.

4. Who or what else from your life is in the picture?
Find each of the elements of your situation in the picture. Trust your intuition. Don't judge your decisions.

5. How can this picture help?
Now you've decided what everything is in the picture, think about how it might help you see the situation differently. Think laterally.

6. What would you like to add or take away from the picture?
For example, you could make all the crows fly away, or change the expression on the scarecrow's face or give him a new outfit..

7. What's next?
Decide on one simple thing you can do in the next seven days that will inspire you to move forward. Write this goal somewhere you'll remember.

*The questions below will guide your thinking. If it helps, get a pad
of paper and write down your answers – remember to date them.*

1. First, decide on what it is you want help with.
Is there a tricky situation you'd like resolving? Or are you looking
for a moment of clarity?

2. Now look at the picture. How does it make you feel?
Does it reflect your situation? Or does it make you think there's a
deeper question you could be asking?

3. Who or what are you in the picture?
You choose. You can be anything, from the scales to one or both
of the candles. You can even be the flame.

4. Who or what else from your life is in the picture?
Find each of the elements of your situation in the picture. Trust your
intuition. Don't judge your decisions.

5. How can this picture help?
Now you've decided what everything is in the picture, think about
how it might help you see the situation differently. Think laterally.

6. What would you like to add or take away from the picture?
For example, you could blow out the lit candle, or light the other one or
dismantle the scales.

7. What's next?
Decide on one simple thing you can do in the next seven days that
will inspire you to move forward. Write this goal somewhere
you'll remember.

The questions below will guide your thinking. If it helps, get a pad of paper and write down your answers – remember to date them.

1. First, decide on what it is you want help with.
Is there a tricky situation you'd like resolving? Or are you looking for a moment of clarity?

2. Now look at the picture. How does it make you feel?
Does it reflect your situation? Or does it make you think there's a deeper question you could be asking?

3. Who or what are you in the picture?
You choose. You can be anything from the man entering the cave to the cave itself or the footsteps. Maybe you're already in the cave.

4. Who or what else from your life is in the picture?
Find each of the elements of your situation in the picture. Trust your intuition. Don't judge your decisions.

5. How can this picture help?
Now you've decided what everything is in the picture, think about how it might help you see the situation differently. Think laterally.

6. What would you like to add or take away from the picture?
For example, you could light up the inside of the cave, add another person to own the footprints, add a chest with a key in the lock or run away.

7. What's next?
Decide on one simple thing you can do in the next seven days that will inspire you to move forward. Write this goal somewhere you'll remember.

The questions below will guide your thinking. If it helps, get a pad of paper and write down your answers – remember to date them.

1. First, decide on what it is you want help with.
Is there a tricky situation you'd like resolving? Or are you looking for a moment of clarity?

2. Now look at the picture. How does it make you feel?
Does it reflect your situation? Or does it make you think there's a deeper question you could be asking?

3. Who or what are you in the picture?
You choose. You can be anything from the blank face to one of the masks or the hands holding them. You could even be in the theatre watching.

4. Who or what else from your life is in the picture?
Find each of the elements of your situation in the picture. Trust your intuition. Don't judge your decisions.

5. How can this picture help?
Now you've decided what everything is in the picture, think about how it might help you see the situation differently. Think laterally.

6. What would you like to add or take away from the picture?
For example, you could throw away the sad mask, cut the woman's hair or give her a face of her own.

7. What's next?
Decide on one simple thing you can do in the next seven days that will inspire you to move forward. Write this goal somewhere you'll remember.

The questions below will guide your thinking. If it helps, get a pad of paper and write down your answers – remember to date them.

1. First, decide on what it is you want help with.
Is there a tricky situation you'd like resolving? Or are you looking for a moment of clarity?

2. Now look at the picture. How does it make you feel?
Does it reflect your situation? Or does it make you think there's a deeper question you could be asking?

3. Who or what are you in the picture?
You choose. You can be anything from one of the people to the signpost or even the letters on the ground.

4. Who or what else from your life is in the picture?
Find each of the elements of your situation in the picture. Trust your intuition. Don't judge your decisions.

5. How can this picture help?
Now you've decided what everything is in the picture, think about how it might help you see the situation differently. Think laterally.

6. What would you like to add or take away from the picture?
For example, you could put the letters back on the sign, add a map to the picture or take the people out of the landscape so you have it to yourself.

7. What's next?
Decide on one simple thing you can do in the next seven days that will inspire you to move forward. Write this goal somewhere you'll remember.

About the authors

Nina Grunfeld is the founding director of a life-coaching business, LifeClubs, which works with individuals and organisations around the world to create happy and confident people who feel resilient and purposeful. She has also had a career as a graphic designer, author, journalist and TV producer. Nina has written 15 books and had columns in *The Daily Telegraph, The Evening Standard* and *Psychologies* Magazine. She has enjoyed reading the *I Ching* regularly since she was a teenager.

Annie Lionnet has written five bestselling books on astrology, Tarot and personal development which have been translated into 11 languages. She also lectures on all aspects of health and well-being. Annie and Nina have known each other since their early twenties and have been collaborating since 2001.

Illustrator **Michael Thomas** was Nina Grunfeld's inspirational graphic design teacher at Harrow College of Art. Together they wrote *Spot Check*, a stain removal guide, that has sold over a million copies worldwide. Under another name Michael is an award-winning illustrator and bestselling author of more than a dozen books.

With thanks to:

Jonathan Goodman, Heather Holden-Brown, Neil Jackson, Thomas Underhill, family and friends and all those who worked at LifeClubs during the writing of this book. And, of course, everyone at Short Books and David Eldridge and Two Associates for the design.